Global Inequalities and the Fair Trade Movement

Global Inequalities and the Fair Trade Movement

Elisabeth Herschbach

MASON CREST
PHILADELPHIA

Mason Crest
450 Parkway Drive, Suite D
Broomall, PA 19008
www.masoncrest.com

©2017 by Mason Crest, an imprint of National Highlights, Inc.

Printed and bound in the United States of America.

CPSIA Compliance Information: Batch #CWI2016.
For further information, contact Mason Crest at 1-866-MCP-Book.

First printing
1 3 5 7 9 8 6 4 2

Library of Congress Cataloging-in-Publication Data

on file at the Library of Congress
ISBN: 978-1-4222-3665-9 (hc)
ISBN: 978-1-4222-8120-8 (ebook)

Understanding Global Trade and Commerce series ISBN: 978-1-4222-3662-8

Table of Contents

KEY ICONS TO LOOK FOR:

Words to Understand: These words with their easy-to-understand definitions will increase the reader's understanding of the text, while building vocabulary skills.

Sidebars: This boxed material within the main text allows readers to build knowledge, gain insights, explore possibilities, and broaden their perspectives by weaving together additional information to provide realistic and holistic perspectives.

Research Projects: Readers are pointed toward areas of further inquiry connected to each chapter. Suggestions are provided for projects that encourage deeper research and analysis.

Text-Dependent Questions: These questions send the reader back to the text for more careful attention to the evidence presented there.

Series Glossary of Key Terms: This back-of-the book glossary contains terminology used throughout this series. Words found here increase the reader's ability to read and comprehend higher-level books and articles in this field.

Most Americans benefit from the lower prices on goods and products that global trade enables. However, due to widespread poverty in many developing countries, young people are often forced to work on farms or in certain industries for low wages, just to help their families survive. These African children are harvesting cotton in Burkina Faso.

Global Trade, Poverty, and Inequality

Global trade has a long history. The ancient Sumerians in Mesopotamia—present-day southern Iraq—imported timber, stone, and metals from as far away as today's Turkey, Afghanistan, and southern Pakistan. Roman-era ships crisscrossed the Mediterranean and beyond, loaded with Egyptian grain, Indian spices, Greek wine, and hundreds of other *lucrative commodities* for trade. Chinese merchants peddled silk and other goods along the Silk Road, a sprawling network of trade routes opened by the Han Dynasty in the second century BCE to link Asia and Europe.

But while international trade is not a new phenomenon, what is new is today's highly integrated global marketplace. For most of human history, trade connections between different continents were limited. Today, every continent is part of a vast web of trade connections, governed by a globalized economy. The food and drinks we consume, the appliances we use, the clothes we wear, and countless other goods and services that we take for granted in everyday life now come from anywhere in the world.

World trade has increased at dramatic rates in recent decades. In 2003, countries around the world exported less than $8 trillion in goods. By 2013, the value of international trade had *surpassed* $18 trillion. Not everyone, however, has benefited to the same degree from today's globalized economy. As a case in point, consider the economics of one of our most popular foods: chocolate.

Everybody Loves Chocolate

Chocolate is the world's best-selling confection, accounting for over 55 percent of all candy sales worldwide. From gourmet bonbons to dollar-store candy bars, more than 7 million tons of chocolate are gobbled up each year around the globe. The Swiss, the world's biggest chocoholics, consume a record-setting twenty-six pounds (12 kg) per person of the sweet treat. That's equivalent to about 240 average-sized chocolate bars. In the United States, a whopping 90 million pounds of chocolate candy are sold during Halloween week alone.

 Words to Understand in This Chapter

accrue—to accumulate over a period of time; to increase in value or amount.

commodity—a product that is bought and sold.

gross domestic product (GDP)—the value of all goods and services produced in a year.

lucrative—profitable; producing or involving great wealth.

surpass—to exceed or do better than.

volatile—subject to change in an extreme or sudden way.

A selection of chocolate snacks on a store shelf in Toronto. The multinational companies Hershey's, Mars, and Nestlé have become the largest manufacturers of chocolate snacks in the world. In recent years, advocates have attempted to pressure these companies into paying a fair price to the cocoa and sugar producers from developing countries that provide the main ingredients for their products.

Our collective sweet tooth means big business for the corporate giants that manufacture our favorite candy brands. Mars Inc., maker of Snickers, M&M's, and many other popular chocolate treats, nets over $18 billion in sales every year. Nestlé SA, another leading chocolate producer, rakes in $10 billion annually. In total, sales from the global chocolate industry top $80 billion a year. But for the farmers who produce the world's supply of cocoa beans—the raw ingredient for chocolate—the deal is not so sweet.

Cocoa beans (opposite) are found within the pods of the cacao tree (above), which grows in tropical rainforest areas such as West Africa, Indonesia, and South America. The process of harvesting and preparing the beans is very labor-intensive.

From Cocoa Bean to Candy Bar

Cocoa beans come from the pods of the cacao tree, a labor-intensive crop that grows only within 15–20 degrees north and south of the equator. A single cacao tree produces about a thousand cocoa beans every year—roughly enough to make two pounds (1 kg) of chocolate.

But before these cocoa beans can end up in a chocolate bar on your local supermarket shelf, they must travel through a long supply chain that runs from farmer to buyer to wholesaler and from exporter to manufacturer to retailer. At each step along the way from pod to bean to candy bar, the product ***accrues*** more value—or profit—on the global market. For this reason, economists refer to the steps in a commodity's supply chain as a value chain.

At the bottom of the chocolate supply chain are the estimated 5 million small-scale farmers who produce the world's cocoa supply. Cocoa farms are scattered across Africa, Asia, and Latin America, but the vast majority of the world's cocoa beans come from just two countries in West Africa: the Ivory Coast and Ghana.

At the top of the supply chain are a handful of large multinational companies that dominate the global cocoa market. Just three manufacturers—Mars, Hershey, and Nestlé—control about 75 percent of the world's total chocolate sales. These corporate titans shape market prices and set the terms of trade. They also capture the lion's share of the profits from the global cocoa industry.

Out of the total price you pay for a candy bar, a tiny fraction—an average of just 4 percent—ends up in the pockets of the cocoa farmers who produce chocolate's essential ingredient. This is a decrease from the 16 percent share that cocoa farmers earned in the 1980s. By contrast, as much as 70 percent of the final price tag goes to the manufacturing companies who produce the name-brand product—up from 56 percent three decades ago.

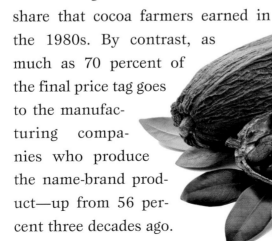

Slaves to Chocolate

Many of us have a sweet spot for chocolate, but there is a dark side to our favorite treat. Cocoa is a highly labor-intensive crop. Yet low incomes often mean that farmers cannot afford to hire extra laborers to help harvest their crops. The result is an industry plagued by the widespread use of child labor.

An estimated 2 million children in West Africa work on cocoa farms, often engaged in dangerous tasks such as operating machinery, lifting heavy loads, and spraying pesticides without protective garments. Many are under twelve years old. Many are deprived of schooling.

Most of these child laborers are working alongside their families. A sizable number of children, however, are slaves, smuggled from neighboring countries and pressed into forced labor on cocoa farms for little or no pay. Tens of thousands of children, some as young as eight, have been sold into slavery by human traffickers in West Africa.

In 2001, after a BBC documentary brought the issue of child slavery on cocoa farms into the international spotlight, the United States adopted the Harkin-Engel Protocol, a voluntary agreement in which large chocolate companies pledged to eradicate child labor from the chocolate industry. The target date for meeting their goal has repeatedly been extended. From an initial deadline of 2005, it was moved to 2008, 2010, and, now, finally, 2020. In the meantime, little has changed in the industry.

A Bitter Harvest

While large-scale corporations reap increasingly big profits from cheap labor and low-cost raw materials, rock-bottom prices in the cocoa industry keep small-scale producers trapped in poverty. They have little bargaining power to negotiate a decent wage. Their livelihoods depend on the ups and downs of a *volatile* market.

The majority of cocoa farmers in West Africa live in

remote villages without reliable access to clean drinking water, electricity, adequate schooling, and basic health care. Their average wage is a mere $2 a day. This leaves them with no resources to invest for the future and no safety net to fall back on when crops fail or natural disasters strike.

Ironically, many West African cocoa farmers don't even know what chocolate tastes like. Although their lives are devoted to cocoa beans, the price of an ordinary candy bar is a luxury beyond reach. West Africa by itself produces almost three-quarters of the world's cocoa supply. Yet the entire continent of Africa accounts for just 3 percent of the world's total chocolate consumption. Wealthy Western

The low wages paid to textile workers in developing countries, such as these Indians, make it possible for Western consumers to purchase inexpensive clothing.

Europe, by contrast, consumes almost half of the world's chocolate.

Global Gap

Sadly, the plight of cocoa farmers is not unusual. Workers on banana plantations in Latin America are often paid as little as $1 a day. They work fourteen-hour shifts and are routinely exposed to dangerous chemical pesticides and fertilizers. Textile workers in Bangladesh are paid $68 a month in sweatshops with poor working conditions. Their counterparts in Ethiopian garment factories fare even worse, earning wages as low as $35 a month. And even though coffee is one of the world's most valuable commodities, the majority of the world's 25 million coffee farmers earn less than $3 a day—roughly the price of one latte.

 Did You Know?

According to a 2000 US State Department report, fifteen thousand children, aged nine to twelve, were sold into forced labor on conventional cotton, coffee, and cocoa plantations in the Ivory Coast.

Overall, some 2.7 billion people live on less than $2 a day, according to the World Bank. That comes to about 40 percent of the world's total population. One billion of the world's citizens live in slums. Some 800 million are malnourished. More than twenty thousand children die every day from poverty-related causes.

The majority of the world's poor are concentrated in sub-Saharan Africa, Central and Latin America, and large parts of Asia. These regions are sometimes referred to as

A farmer in Thailand gathers the fruit of oil palms for sale. Palm oil is widely used in the commercial food industry throughout the world.

the "Global South" because of their location in the southern hemisphere. North America, Western Europe, Australia, and parts of East Asia—home to the world's most developed nations—are collectively known as the "Global North."

In economic terms, the gap between the Global South and the Global North is stark. The countries of the Global North make up a quarter of the world's population. Yet they control 80 percent of the world's income, own 90 percent of the world's manufacturing industries, and account for 70 percent of all international trade.

By contrast, the economies of the Global South depend disproportionately on industries at the bottom of the value chain, such as the production of low-priced commodities. For example, nearly half the population in the Ivory Coast earns a living from cocoa production. Burundi, ranked fifth from the bottom on the United Nations Human Development Index, depends on coffee for 54 percent of its total exports.

To Market, To Market

The world's poor face enormous challenges, including high rates of malnutrition and disease; poor infrastructure; geographical isolation; and lack of access to computers, telephones, transportation, and the Internet. These challenges can make it difficult to participate in the global economy at all.

Most economists agree that increased trade is the key to reducing poverty and improving the economic prospects of the Global South. There is disagreement, however, about what principles and practices should govern international trade.

Free trade proponents argue that free market mechanisms, based on more open and unregulated economic exchange, will raise incomes and reduce poverty worldwide. Critics argue that the world's poorest nations need not just more free trade, but fairer trade—trade that provides a sustainable living wage. This criticism has inspired the fair trade movement, a growing consumer movement to make the global market more equitable.

 Text-Dependent Questions

1. What is a value chain?
2. What percentage of the world's population lives on less than $2 a day?
3. What do the terms "Global South" and "Global North" refer to?

 Research Project

Look at the 2014 UN Human Development Index (http://hdr.undp.org/en/composite/HDI). Identify the three top-ranked and three lowest-ranked countries on the index and compare them in terms of gross national income (GNI), life expectancy, and mean years of schooling. Conduct some independent research of your own and find out more about the economic profiles of these countries, including their top industries, main exports, and gross domestic product (GDP). Present your findings to your class.

The rise of global trade networks over the past half-century has improved the standard of living for millions of people. However, despite economic growth many people in the developing world are still living in poverty.

2

The Fair Trade Movement

Globalization has brought Western consumers an *unprecedented* range of cheap goods from all over the world—from tropical commodities, like coffee and cocoa, to high-tech gadgets and electronics assembled from components manufactured around the globe.

But fair trade advocates argue that the cheap prices we have come to expect conceal hidden costs. Big corporations capitalize on cheap labor from developing countries and environmentally unsustainable practices to keep consumer prices low and their own profits high. Meanwhile, the world's poorest citizens shoulder a disproportionate share of both the social and the environmental costs. According to a 2009 Global Humanitarian Forum report, 98 percent of the people most severely impacted by climate change live in developing countries.

The goal of the fair trade movement is to help disadvantaged farmers and producers in the Global South by establishing trade relationships based on more favorable terms. Fair trade programs guarantee a higher price for products—a price that covers the costs of production with something left over for investment in the community. They promote better working conditions and higher environmental standards. And they work to expand the market for fairly traded products by educating consumers about the costs of conventional trade.

How we spend our money, fair trade proponents argue, can directly impact the lives of impoverished workers in the developing world.

Fair Trade's Early Days

Consumer movements for ethical trade are not new. Eighteenth-century abolitionists in Britain launched a mass boycott against sugar grown by slaves in the Caribbean, then Britain's biggest import. Some 400,000 people joined

 Words to Understand in This Chapter

boom and bust cycle—a cycle of economic expansion and contraction.

economy of scale—a reduction in the cost of producing something that comes from increasing the size of production facilities.

mitigate—to soften or reduce the effect of something; to make less severe.

monocroppping—the agricultural practice of growing a single crop on the same land every year, instead of rotating through different crops or planting multiple crops on the same land.

unprecedented—never done, seen, or experienced before.

Unjust Java

The Max Havelaar fair trade certification label gets its name from a nineteenth-century Dutch novel by Eduard Douwes Dekker, a disillusioned government employee who served in Indonesia during the Dutch colonial period. Writing under the pen name Multatuli—Latin for "I have suffered greatly"—Dekker chronicled the exploitation and mistreatment of Indonesian coffee growers and drew international attention to the abuses of colonial rule.

Under a Dutch government policy designed to boost that government's revenues, farmers in Java and other parts of Indonesia were forced to grow a quota of cash crops for export—such as coffee, tobacco, and sugar—instead of staple foods like rice. They were also forced to hand over a portion of their agricultural harvests to the Dutch government as a land tax. These policies significantly increased Dutch profits from exports. For Indonesians, however, the result was increased poverty and starvation.

Dekker's novel is credited with playing a direct role in shaming the Dutch government into reforming some of its worst colonial abuses. It also vividly highlights the way in which past legacies of conquest, colonization, and exploitation have shaped the current global order and the circumstances of the world's poorest nations.

the boycott at its peak. Sugar sales from the Caribbean plummeted by over a third in just a few months. Sales of sugar grown without slave labor in Southeast Asia grew tenfold.

The roots of the modern fair trade movement go back to the late 1940s, when several nonprofits and church organizations began importing and selling handicrafts from impoverished artisans to help raise their standard of living.

In 1946, Kansas businesswoman Edna Ruth Byler, a

Sign outside an Oxfam charity shop in Berkshire, England. The organization was originally founded during the Second World War as the Oxford Committee for Famine Relief, and was intended to help people in countries that were devastated by the conflict. Today, Oxfam is an international confederation of 17 organizations that work to reduce poverty and improve social justice in more than 90 countries worldwide.

member of the Mennonite Church, began buying textiles hand-sewn by cash-strapped Puerto Rican craftswomen and selling them to friends and family out of the trunk of her car. Byler soon expanded her focus to helping needy artisans from a broader range of developing regions. Eventually, her grassroots initiative blossomed into the well-known fair trade retail outlet Ten Thousand Villages.

In 1948, Oxfam, an organization founded by British Quakers to raise funds for famine victims in war-torn

Europe, opened its first charity shop to sell fair trade products. Several other organizations followed suit with the same goal of creating a fair marketplace for the products of disadvantaged artisans from around the world.

Putting a Label On It

Fair trade products were originally available only in specialized retail outlets, such as church shops, nonprofit organizations, food co-ops, mail-order catalogs, and special stores called worldshops that sell only fair-trade goods. In the 1980s, however, the focus of the fair trade movement shift-

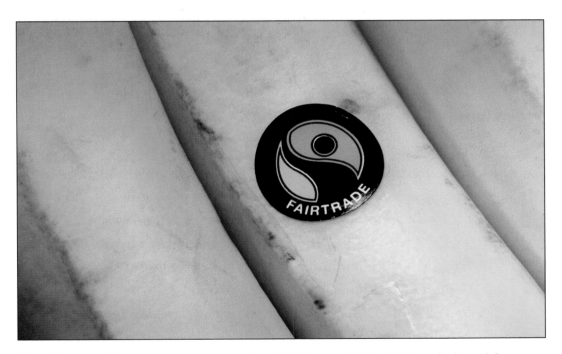

These imported bananas on a grocery store shelf bear a Fairtrade Foundation sticker. Founded in 1992, the Fairtrade Foundation is a British charity that certifies that certain agricultural products, such as bananas and coffee, have been produced according to international fair trade standards.

Workers harvest a sugar cane crop in northeastern Thailand.

ed to certifying and labeling products for sale in mainstream venues like supermarkets.

Fueling this shift in orientation were coffee beans from a Mexican coffee cooperative called Union of the Indigenous Communities of the Isthmus Region (Unión de Comunidades Indígenas de la Región del Istmo, or UCIRI). In 1988, the Dutch development agency Solidaridad partnered with UCIRI to help establish a stable and fair-priced retail market for their coffee beans. The result was the Max Havelaar certification label, the world's first fair trade consumer label.

The brand captured almost 3 percent of the Dutch coffee market in just three months. In just two years, UCIRI saw its coffee sales rise tenfold, and it expanded its exports to over twelve countries, including the United States and Canada.

Setting a Standard

Following on the heels of Max Havelaar's success, similar fair trade certification initiatives soon cropped up around the world. From just a handful of products—primarily handicrafts and coffee—the range of fair trade items available to socially conscious consumers expanded to a wide selection of other products, including tea, cocoa, fruit, honey, sugar, and spices.

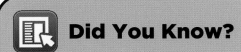

Did You Know?

In 2012, 163 million pounds (74 million kg) of fair trade–certified coffee were imported into the United States and Canada—an 18 percent jump from the previous year.

The largest umbrella organization for setting fair trade certification and labeling standards is Fairtrade International (FLO). Currently, FLO oversees labeling initiatives in twenty-five countries, including Canada, Australia, New Zealand, Japan, and eighteen European nations. While Fair Trade USA was originally part of the FLO system, it became independent from FLO in 2011.

Specific products have their own specific certification criteria, but all certified fair trade products must meet certain core standards and minimum requirements. These standards are aimed at *mitigating* the disadvantages that the world's poorest farmers and producers face in conventional markets.

Negotiating a Fair Deal

Giant multinational corporations at the top of the conventional supply chain can manipulate market prices to their advantage. But disempowered farmers and producers at the bottom of the chain are hostage to unpredictable market

Handlers from Cooperative Café Timor are seen sifting coffee beans. With 21,500 members, Cooperative Café Timor is the largest employer in the nation of East Timor during the coffee season.

patterns and roller-coaster *cycles of boom and bust*.

In contrast to conventional trade, however, fair trade guarantees a stable price that protects small producers from the ups and downs of international markets. Fair trade buyers and producers negotiate together to fix a mutually agreed-upon price, calculated on the basis of production costs and the cost of living. In addition, fair trade buyers pay a social premium—an extra sum of money on top of the floor price. This social premium is used to fund community projects, such as health clinics, schools, and better roads.

Fair trade buyers also offer farmers credit, which may take the form of prepayment for up to 60 percent of a contract. This can be a lifeline for poor farmers, who often struggle to make it from harvest to harvest. Outside of the fair trade system, many small-scale farmers have trouble getting financing and fall victim to predatory lenders who impose unfair repayment conditions, perpetuating the cycle of poverty and debt.

Cutting Out the Middleman

Conventional trade involves a long chain of intermediaries, or "middlemen." Wholesalers, exporters, importers, shippers, distributors, and retailers all take a cut from the final price of a product. By the time all these intermediaries have taken their share, only a sliver of the overall price makes it back to the farmer—and often not until many months later.

Local traders—called "coyotes" in Latin America—add an extra link to the already long chain of intermediaries in the conventional supply chain. Small-scale farmers typically do not produce large enough quantities of their crops to meet the volume requirements for world trading. As a result, they must rely on local traders to act as middlemen.

These middlemen buy harvests from many different small farmers and combine them into large shipments to sell to exporters, keeping a percentage of each farmer's profits for themselves. They often pay below-market prices, knowing that disadvantaged farmers have no leverage, or bargaining power, and can't afford the luxury of waiting for a better deal. Some unscrupulous middlemen even use rigged scales to weigh the produce of farmers who are too poor to afford a scale of their own.

Fair trade organizations try to address these problems by eliminating unnecessary intermediaries and establishing more direct trade connections between farmers and distributors. With fewer intermediaries taking a cut of the profits, farmers are left with a higher share of the market price.

Safeguarding Workers

One way that fair trade organizations try to cut out the middleman is by requiring farmers to be organized into cooperatives or collectives. Joining a cooperative allows small farmers to pool their harvests so that they can sell directly to distributors without having to rely on a middleman. It also enables them to pool their resources to buy much-needed equipment, to share costs, and to reduce their overhead by taking advantage of *economies of scale.*

Under fair trade standards, cooperatives are required to be democratically organized, to divide profits equitably among all members, and to observe certain minimum safeguards for worker rights, including worker safety standards, a commitment to nondiscrimination, and a rejection of child labor.

Respecting the Environment

In addition to setting standards for fair labor practices, the fair trade movement requires producers to meet certain baseline standards for environmental protection. Fair trade organizations encourage the use of ecologically sound practices, including crop rotation, reforestation, sustainable management of raw materials, and reduction of energy con-

African workers collect tea leaves on a plantation in Rwanda.

sumption and greenhouse gas emissions. And although fair trade certification does not necessarily mean that a product has been organically grown, most fair trade producers try to avoid the use of chemical fertilizers and pesticides.

The fair trade commitment to environmentally sustainable practices stands in sharp contrast to prevailing trends in conventional agriculture. To boost crop production, industrial farming makes heavy use of chemical pesticides and fertilizers—substances that have been linked to a number of human health risks, including birth defects, cancer, hormonal disorders, and cognitive disabilities. Worldwide, more than 5 billion pounds (2.3 billion kg) of fertilizers and pesticides are used every year on conventionally grown crops. Up to 250 pounds (114 kg) per acre (0.4 ha) of agrochemicals are used on coffee alone.

 Did You Know?

More pesticides are used on cotton than on any other single crop—about 16 percent of the total amount used in agriculture as a whole. In total, the global cotton industry spends $2 billion a year on pesticides. More than $800 million of that total goes to chemicals classified as hazardous by the World Health Organization.

Vast ecosystems, including tropical rain forests, are destroyed to make way for intensive *monocropping*. An estimated 6 million acres (2.4 million ha) of land have been cleared in the Ivory Coast to plant more cacao trees; that's an area only slightly smaller than the size of Nova Scotia. Almost 10 million acres (4 million ha) of forests are destroyed every year in South America. More than half of that destruction occurs in

Brazil's Amazon rain forest—a crucial ecosystem for fighting climate change because it can absorb large amounts of carbon dioxide.

These ecologically destructive practices cause soil and water contamination, air pollution, erosion, depletion of soil nutrients, decreased biodiversity, and a long list of other environmental problems. And, according to some labor and environmental activists, these problems are a result of the increasingly unregulated global markets favored by free trade policies.

 Text-Dependent Questions

1. What was the first product to get fair trade certification?
2. What does the term "coyote" refer to?
3. What are some of the goals of the fair trade movement, and how does this movement distinguish fair trade from conventional trade?

 Research Project

Browse through your local supermarket and make note of the different types of fair trade products that are available. How do the fair trade versions compare to the conventional versions in terms of price and other features that consumers care about? One goal of the fair trade movement is to raise awareness among Western consumers about the conditions of trade, including where our consumer goods come from and how they are produced. Choose one of the fair trade brands available at your supermarket. Find out as much as you can from the product packaging or from an Internet search about the livelihoods of the producers, and write a report about it.

A 2008 study by the UN's International Labour Organization of seventy-three countries found that about two-thirds have experienced growing income inequality. In some countries, the gap between the richest and poorest people has increased by more than 170 percent over the past two decades.

3

Free Trade
and Its Critics

Every country in the world imposes some restrictions on trade, whether in the form of taxes, *subsidies*, price controls, or government regulations. Over the past several decades, however, reducing restrictions on international trade—a process that economists refer to as "trade liberalization"—has become the dominant approach to economic development.

Today, international trade agreements promote trade liberalization by pushing for policies aimed at opening markets to international trade and private investment. These policies include reducing *tariffs* and *quotas* on imports, cutting domestic subsidies, encouraging foreign investment and the privatization of state-owned industries, eliminating price controls, and decreasing government regulation. These policies are based on the view that free trade and free markets are the best way to stimulate economic growth around the globe.

While free trade policies started to gain ascendance in the 1970s and 1980s, they are rooted in ideas that are almost two-and-a-half centuries old—ideas that stem from the work of an eighteenth-century Scottish philosopher named Adam Smith.

Free Markets and the Wealth of Nations

In 1776, Adam Smith published a nine-hundred-page *tome* that set out to explain what makes nations prosper economically. Written at the beginning of the Industrial Revolution, *An Inquiry into the Nature and Causes of the Wealth of Nations* sought to provide a new economic theory to replace what Smith saw as outdated systems of thought no longer relevant to the changing world order.

One of Smith's main targets was the theory of mercantilism, the prevailing economic theory of his day. Mercantilists advocated government restrictions on trade,

 Words to Understand in This Chapter

multilateral—involving more than two groups or countries.

quota—a specific limit on the number or amount of something that is allowed.

subsidy—money, usually paid by a government, used to keep a product's price low.

tariff—a tax or duty imposed by a government on a particular class of imports or exports.

tome—a very large, thick book.

such as import taxes, subsidies, and government-licensed monopolies to control the flow of goods and services. This is because they believed that nations prosper economically by amassing as much wealth as possible within their borders. For the mercantilists, this meant that each nation should try to maximize its exports while importing as little as possible from other nations. In this way, nations would bring in more income without letting it flow out.

Smith argued, however, that it is counterproductive to try to limit imports and restrict trade between nations. Instead, he contended, the key to economic growth and prosperity lies in unrestricted trade across borders—in other words, in a system of free trade and free markets.

According to Smith, free trade promotes economic growth because it increases competition, which forces industries and businesses to be optimally efficient. In turn, efficiency boosts productivity, and increased productivity translates into bigger profits. As the global economy grows through increased production and trade, people will become more prosperous and will use their extra income to buy more goods, thus stimulating more trade in an ongoing cycle of economic growth.

French Wine and Scottish Wool

To illustrate his point, Smith used the example of wine production in Scotland. Thanks to its wet, cold climate, Scotland is not a very good place to grow grapes. Although grapes can be grown in a hothouse, the extra cost of heating and maintenance adds a significant expense to the overall cost of production. As a result, wine is more costly to make in Scotland than in France, where the climate and soil conditions are perfect for cultivating grapes.

To protect its domestic wine industry, Scotland could use import controls, subsidies, and other government interventions to shield it from French competition. According to Smith, however, it makes more economic sense to let the forces of market competition naturally weed out industries—like Scottish winemaking—that are not cost-effective.

Instead of wasting its resources on producing wine, Scotland should focus on producing the commodities that it can make more profitably—such as wool from its abundant sheep farms. In turn, it should eliminate high tariffs on international imports so that other goods—such as wine—can be brought in cheaply from abroad. If Scotland exports its wool to France and France exports its wine to Scotland under a system of free trade, then both countries stand to benefit. Consumers in both countries will profit from being able to buy lower-priced goods. And the economies of both nations will profit from having expanded markets beyond their borders where they can sell more of their products.

Free Trade Today

Adam Smith's economic theory is based on the idea that open competition and unregulated markets promote efficiency, productivity, and increased wealth around the world. Today, this core idea forms the basis for the economic policies of three powerful financial institutions that govern the global economy: the World Trade Organization (WTO), the International Monetary Fund (IMF), and the World Bank.

The World Bank and the IMF were created in 1944, as part of a strategy to help rebuild nations ravaged by World War II. The World Bank finances projects for long-term economic development. The International Monetary Fund lends money to debt-ridden countries in danger of defaulting on loans. The WTO, created in 1995, grew out of the

 ## Corporations First?

Writing at a time when only a small fraction of people in Britain had the right to vote, Adam Smith was concerned about how undemocratic governments can use their power to support the interests of a wealthy minority. As he observed, trade barriers, such as import controls, can be used to cater to special interests, such as powerful industry lobbies.

But critics argue that trade barriers can also serve legitimate functions. These include protecting food supplies, promoting equitable income distribution, and safeguarding worker rights and the environment. Critics today warn that deregulation of the market has granted a monopoly of power to multinational corporations that use their clout to undermine protections put in place by democratically elected governments.

Government regulations aimed at protecting workers or the environment are often treated as barriers to free trade and struck down by the WTO and other free trade organizations. In one of its first rulings, the WTO sided with Venezuela and Brazil in a 1996 case against a US Environmental Protection Agency regulation requiring cleaner oil. The regulation, the WTO argued, amounted to unfair trade discrimination against imports into the United States. In 1997, the US-based company Ethyl Corporation sued Canada for its ban on the gasoline additive MMT, a neurotoxin, using NAFTA guidelines. The Canadian government paid a $13 million settlement. Such examples fuel the criticism that free trade agreements put corporate interests above the welfare of people and the environment.

In the 1980s, free market economics found its staunchest champions in US President Ronald Reagan and British Prime Minister Margaret Thatcher. Reagan's cabinet members were known to wear ties emblazoned with Adam Smith's portrait. In her speeches and interviews, Thatcher repeated the mantra that there is no alternative to free market capitalism so often that commentators started shortening "There is no alternative" to the acronym TINA.

General Agreement on Tariffs and Trade (GATT), a *multilateral* treaty signed in 1947 to set rules for international trade.

Together, these three international economic organizations push for trade liberalization. The WTO oversees trade negotiations between its 162 member-states, promoting policies favoring privatization, deregulation, and the expansion of global trade and investment. The IMF and the World Bank reinforce the WTO's agenda by making free market reforms a condition for obtaining loans and development aid.

In addition to the broad, multilateral agreements negotiated by the WTO, there are some 350 regional trade agreements operating on a smaller scale around the world. Essentially, these regional agreements set up trading blocs, or free trade zones, between a select set of countries in order to facilitate open trade. In 1993, for example, the United States, Canada, and Mexico signed the North American Free Trade Agreement (NAFTA), lowering protectionist trade barriers between the three nations. Other examples of regional trade agreements in operation today are the European Union, the European Free Trade

American businessman Bill Gates is among the world's wealthiest people, with a fortune of about $80 billion. The combined net worth of the twenty richest people in the world is more than the total combined GDP of the world's forty-nine least-developed countries.

Association (EFTA), the Common Market for Eastern and Southern Africa (COMESA), and the Association of Southeast Asian Nations (ASEAN).

Spreading the Wealth?

The past few decades have seen enormous increases in global trade and an unprecedented rise in overall wealth. In the half century between 1950 and 2000, global trade grew twentyfold. Since 2000 alone, the world's total household wealth has doubled. At the same time, the global poverty rate has plummeted. In 1981, 44 percent of the world's population earned $1.90 a day or less. By 2012, the global poverty rate had dropped to 12.7 percent.

According to free trade theorists, these trends are proof that the dominant policies of the past few decades really work. Trade liberalization, they argue, boosts the global economy by increasing the volume of world trade. In turn, this economic growth trickles down to the world's poor, raising incomes and standards of living around the globe.

Skeptics, however, argue that the statistics obscure a crucial fact: most of the dramatic decrease in world poverty since 1980 occurred in just a handful of East Asian countries, particularly China. And, for the most part, the economic success stories are nations that have largely bucked the trend of trade liberalization. China, for example, slashed its poverty rate from 85 percent in 1981 to 15 percent in 2005 while implementing the kinds of protectionist measures frowned on by free trade advocates. These measures include high tariffs to build their industrial base, regulations on foreign investment, and resistance to wholesale privatization.

By contrast, Africa, Latin America, Eastern Europe, and Central Asia have largely seen their living standards stagnate. The poverty rate in sub-Saharan Africa—where the World Bank and the IMF imposed a strict program of structural reforms in the 1990s—remains stuck at 50 percent. The absolute number of poor has increased from 200 million in 1981 to more than 400 million today. Across forty-three African countries, the average income actually shrank by one-fourth between 1990 and 2000.

Winners and Losers

According to critics, trade liberalization has not delivered the benefits that free trade theorists claim—especially for the poorest countries of the world. Economic growth has

Although free-trade agreements like NAFTA have created economic growth, many people are opposed to them because they fear a loss of jobs to lower-income countries. These Canadians are protesting in Toronto against the proposed Trans-Pacific Partnership Agreement (TPP) in January 2016.

been highly uneven across countries. While income levels have increased exponentially in some parts of the world, so has the gap between the world's richest and poorest countries. In 1987, the per capita GDP of the United States was twenty-six times the combined per capita GDP of the world's least-developed countries. Today, it is more than fifty times higher.

Meanwhile, the wealth gap has widened not just between but also within countries. Although the net wealth of the world's richest countries has ballooned, the way that this income is distributed has become increasingly unequal. In the United States, the average CEO earns more than 520 times as much as the average employee, up from 370 times as much just four years ago. Since 1980, the wealthiest 1 percent of Americans have doubled their share of the national income from 10 percent to 20 percent.

In Canada, the average CEO's salary is 184 times higher than that of the average worker. The richest 1 percent of Canadians have seen their share of the national wealth grow from 8 percent in 1982 to more than 13 percent in 2010. In that same period, the poorest 10 percent of Canadians have seen their median net worth shrink by 150 percent.

Did You Know?

Howard Schultz, the CEO of Starbucks, the largest coffee chain in the world, received a total compensation of $21.5 million in 2014. That's equal to the annual income of more than 39,000 Ethiopians coffee industry workers.

The same trend is evident around the globe, as more and more of the world's wealth is becoming concentrated in the hands of the ultra-rich. Today, the wealthiest three hundred people on the planet have more income than the poorest 3 billion combined. All together, the richest 10 percent own 88 percent of the world's wealth. The top 1 percent own half of all the income in the world.

According to critics of free trade, the gulf between the haves and the have-nots is growing in large part because of the economic policies promoted by the international financial institutions and trade agreements shaping our global economy. Instead of ushering in a new era of prosperity benefiting everybody, these policies have perpetuated an economic system of winners and losers—thanks to global markets that prioritize corporate profits over fair living standards.

 ## Text-Dependent Questions

1. According to Adam Smith, why are import tariffs, quotas, and other trade barriers counterproductive?
2. What are the functions of the WTO, the IMF, and the World Bank?
3. Over the past few decades, what have been the trends in income distribution, both between and within countries?

 ## Research Project

Using resources in your library or on the Internet, learn more about the effects of NAFTA on the United States, Canada, and Mexico in terms of jobs, wages, environmental laws, living standards, and economic growth. Based on your findings, do you think that NAFTA has brought more gains or losses for the three nations? Write a one-page paper justifying your answer.

A Laotian farmer uses a vintage machine to remove the hulls from coffee beans. Fair trade policies enable small farmers to earn a living wage while competing with large producers.

4

Free Trade
versus Fair Trade

Adam Smith, the father of free market capitalism, advocated unregulated trade because he believed in the power of free markets to promote the collective good—a process he described using the metaphor of an invisible hand. Left unimpeded, the forces of supply and demand will lead to the most efficient distribution of resources for everyone, as if being guided invisibly. By contrast, according to Smith, deliberate attempts to steer the market through government intervention are harmful because they distort the natural equilibrium of the marketplace.

Critics today, however, argue that free trade theorists overlook the way that unequal power dynamics derail the workings of Smith's invisible hand. When poor, weak nations are forced to compete with wealthy, powerful nations on an uneven playing field, free trade policies simply perpetuate an unequal status quo. Wealthy nations with advanced industries prosper, while poor nations with underdeveloped economies remain trapped on the bottom rung of the global economy.

Unequal Partners

As we saw in chapter 1, the wealthy nations of the Global North enjoy a disproportionate share of the world's *assets*, accounting for four-fifths of the world's wealth. This means that they exert a disproportionate influence over the global economic order. All too often, the world's richest nations use this clout to shape the rules of the global economy to their advantage

In theory, the World Trade Organization is supposed to promote a level playing field in the arena of international trade. It establishes a set of common rules that apply to all members equally, and its governing structure is democratic in the sense that each country gets one vote. Because developing nations have the numerical advantage, their voice

 Words to Understand in This Chapter

asset—an economically valuable item owned by a person or company.

culvert—a structure or pipe that allows water from a stream to flow under a road or a trail.

precarious—uncertain, risky, hazardous, or insecure.

prefinancing—money paid in advance by customers to help finance a project.

regime—a government or a system of rule.

tangible—having real substance; capable of being clearly grasped by the mind or felt.

should count more in negotiations. In reality, however, WTO decisions are never made on the basis of votes. Instead, the organization is controlled by a small group of powerful nations. Important negotiations take place behind closed doors in meetings that are by invitation only.

As a result, many of the WTO's rules are strongly biased toward the interests of the richest and most powerful nations. These rules tend to favor free trade in areas where rich countries already have an advantage, but not in areas where they are weaker. For example, while the WTO bans most domestic subsidies, it allows developed nations to continue subsidizing agriculture and textile production. Every year, the world's wealthy nations hand out some $100 billion in subsidies to their farmers. The United States alone shells out $4 billion a year on peanut-farm subsidies.

For poor nations, this double standard often has devastating effects. Farm subsidies can lead to oversupply, deflating prices in the world market and severely cutting into the livelihoods of already impoverished farmers in the Global South. India, for example, claims that US cotton subsidies have cost its own cotton industry more than $1 billion in revenues. Oxfam estimates that cutting all cotton subsidies would bump up world cotton prices by as much as 14 percent.

Past Injustices, Present Inequalities

Today's imbalances of power both reflect and reinforce inequalities from the past. For many former colonies, a brutal history of colonization and exploitation has left a legacy of poverty, political instability, weak government institutions, technological backwardness, and economic underdevelopment.

In many cases, colonial *regimes* actively discouraged their colonies from industrializing to protect their own economies from competition. Colonies were pushed into producing cash crops and raw materials—the commodities at the lowest end of the value chain. These low-priced commodities became the basis for their entire economies.

In the era of free trade, the dynamics of the global supply chain put these nations at a severe disadvantage. Because profit is concentrated in the hands of manufacturers at the top end of the chain, global trade represents an unequal exchange for the producers at the bottom.

According to critics, the free trade agenda of the past few decades has done little to even out this imbalance. Instead, the financial institutions and trade agreements that drive the global economy have simply placed more wealth and power in the hands of multinational corporations. In turn, these multinationals have undermined safeguards for workers, consumers, and the environment in a bid to compete for the cheapest labor and the lowest overhead costs.

Making Free Trade Fairer

The fair trade movement, as we saw in chapter 2, is an attempt to level the playing field for marginalized producers in the developing world. Fair trade programs try to accomplish this by offering a fairer price, a social premium for

The Oromoa Farmers Cooperative in Ethiopia used funds from its fair trade premiums to build a community school, which now enrolls more than a thousand students.

community investment, more direct trading connections, access to credit and *prefinancing*, and better working conditions and environmental standards. The basic idea is that more equitable trading conditions can help impoverished producers in the Global South climb the economic ladder to a position of greater financial security.

But although the fair trade movement tries to correct some of the imbalances in the global marketplace, it is not opposed to free trade. Instead, it operates within the free market system, using voluntary, market-based strategies to

In October 2012, the American chocolate company Hershey's announced that it would transition to using only Fair Trade-certified cocoa in its products by 2020. Advocates of fair trade were pleased with the announcement, though they noted that the company had not yet ruled out the use of non-certified sugar in Hershey's chocolates and candy.

accomplish its goals, as opposed to regulations and state policy. Fair trade certification labels work the same way as the organic certification system: consumers pay a higher price to cover the costs of sustainable production. In return, they get products that are certified to meet certain minimum standards.

By mobilizing consumer awareness, fair trade organizations try to nudge the global marketplace toward more advantageous conditions for producers in developing nations. Over time, it is hoped, market demands will respond to growing consumer awareness. As consumers come to understand the hidden costs associated with the low prices of conventional goods, there will be less demand for lower-priced goods. As a result, market prices will shift upward to reflect the real costs of production.

A Sweeter Deal

Some 80 percent of the world's sugar comes from small-scale sugarcane producers in tropical countries such as Belize, Costa Rica, Malawi, Paraguay, and the Philippines. Their livelihoods are *precarious* and difficult. Typically, they earn a mere $1–5 a day. They labor long hours under harsh working conditions, facing health risks, including heat stroke from the hot tropical sun and exposure to toxins from chemical pesticides, herbicides, and fertilizers. A highly volatile market brings drastic price swings, and already low prices are driven even lower by European subsidies to sugar beet farmers.

For one sugar-producing cooperative in a remote corner of rural Paraguay, however, fair trade has brought sweet success. In 1999, a group of sugarcane farmers in Paraguay's Arroyos y Esteros district joined together to form a cooperative and gain fair trade certification. The Manduvirá cooperative became the first in Paraguay to export its own sugar directly to overseas markets.

Using the money they earned from fair trade premiums, they built their own sugar mill in 2011. This means that they no longer have to pay to transport their sugarcane to a mill more than 62 miles (100 km) away. It also puts them on the path to financial self-sufficiency. From small-scale growers of sugarcane, they have become producers of processed sugar.

Today, Manduvirá has more than fifteen hundred members. They export to more than thirty clients around the world. They have also expanded the range of their crops to include cotton, molasses, sesame, and stevia.

A Price That Pays

Because there is no standardized evaluation process for all fair trade initiatives, it is difficult to quantify the overall successes of the movement. However, a number of studies and surveys conducted by organizations affiliated with the World Fair Trade Organization (WFTO) have shown that fair trade is having a meaningful impact on producers in developing countries. One of the most *tangible* benefits is the higher income guaranteed by the fair trade minimum pricing system.

Especially for farmers producing tropical commodities, like coffee, cocoa beans, and cotton—where conventional prices are low and the market is very volatile—the higher fair trade price can mean the difference between bankruptcy and survival. In Mexico, for example, surveys have shown that the price for fair trade coffee averages twice the street price that conventional local buyers pay. Even when market prices for coffee plummeted during the coffee crisis of 1999–2005, bankrupting tens of thousands of small-scale farmers, fair trade prices remained as much as three times higher than conventional prices.

Fair trade prices have also been shown to have a spin-off effect on conventional market prices. In Mexico, conven-

 Did You Know?

Between 1996 and 2003, the price of cotton dropped by 55 percent, thanks to oversupplies in global cotton production and the dumping of cheap cotton imports by subsidized nations. In India, the world's second-largest cotton producer, an estimated 300,000 bankrupt cotton farmers committed suicide between 1995 and 2011.

Shoppers browse the fruit stalls at a market in Rio de Janeiro, Brazil. Studies indicate that fair trade prices for exported fruits and vegetables can also help to increase what farmers receive when they sell their produce locally.

tional street traders have bumped up their rates to compete with the higher prices available to farmers through fair trade networks. There is evidence of a similar dynamic taking place in many other countries as well, including Bolivia, Peru, Nicaragua, Ghana, and Tanzania.

Moving Up the Ladder

For impoverished nations in the Global South, the key to economic growth is to develop more advanced industries that allow workers to move further up the supply chain—

from producing low-end raw materials to exporting high-end manufactured goods. For many producers in developing countries, the fair trade premium can serve as a step up to the next rung on the ladder.

As we saw in chapter 2, the social premium is an extra sum of money earmarked for community investment projects, paid on top of the regular fair trade price. The amount of the premium is fixed by specific certification organizations on a product-by-product basis. For coffee, for example, Fairtrade International sets the premium at 20 cents per pound (2 kg). In 2011, the total Fairtrade premium paid to coffee producers around the world came to $84 million.

Ultimately, producer cooperatives on the ground can decide to use social premium funds any way they like. Typically, however, the funds are channeled into projects that raise living standards and improve their businesses. These projects include building training centers and schools, investing in new equipment and machinery, and improving farming practices.

Some producers use the extra funds to convert to organic farming, which not only is more environmentally sustainable but also pays farmers more. Others invest in much-needed infrastructure, such as better water storage facilities, waste management systems, and animal-proof fences. In Nueva York, Peru, members of the women's coffee cooperative Café Femenino used social premium funds to finance the construction of a *culvert* in 2012.

Such improvements may seem small, but they make a big difference to cash-strapped farmers struggling to make ends meet. Gradually, these small improvements add up to increased productivity and efficiency, helping farmers to expand their operations and gain better incomes. In some cases, small-scale producers have been able to use the fair trade premium to make the jump from producing raw materials to exporting processed goods. For example, members of the Gumutindo coffee cooperative in Uganda have used fair trade funds to construct their own coffee processing mill, thus taking more control over the production process.

 ## Text-Dependent Questions

1. According to critics, how do the WTO's policies perpetuate and reinforce pre-existing inequalities in the world order?
2. What is the relationship between the fair trade movement and the free market system?
3. What are some ways that the fair trade premium is used by producer cooperatives?

 ## Research Project

Conduct a poll of your friends and family. How many are aware of the fair trade movement? How many are willing to pay extra for fair trade products that come with a guarantee of a more equitable standard of trade that improves the livelihoods of producers in the developing world? Compile the results of your survey and present your findings to your class.

While fair trade sales are enjoying enormous growth, the number of certified producers around the world is also expanding. According to some estimates, up to 30 percent of small-scale coffee farmers around the world are now linked to fair trade networks.

5

Does Fair Trade Work?

Fair trade started out as an obscure niche movement, with a narrow range of products available only through select outlets, such as worldshops, charity shops, church bazaars, and mail-order companies. Today, fair trade is a globally recognized label with a long list of products—including coffee, tea, chocolate, bananas, honey, sugar, spices, nuts, cotton, quinoa, rice, wine, beer, and even soccer balls—that can be found in many major stores.

More than thirty thousand fair trade products are now sold in 125 countries around the world. These goods are produced by over a million farmers and other workers who belong to more than a thousand producer organizations in 74 countries around the world. And, as we saw in chapter 4, study after study has shown that fair trade has improved the lives of these workers in measurable ways.

Criticisms of Fair Trade

Despite evidence that fair trade makes a difference in the lives of small-scale farmers in the Global South, the fair trade movement is not without its *detractors*. Some critics complain that there is no mechanism in place for determining how much of the extra price consumers pay actually reaches the producers, instead of being pocketed by the companies. Others argue that the use of a guaranteed minimum price impedes the efficient functioning of the free market by keeping prices artificially high.

One of the most persistent lines of criticism is that the requirements involved in the fair trade certification process are too costly for the world's poorest producers. Fair trade producers have to pay both an initial certification fee, which varies depending on the size of their operation, and an annual flat fee. These fees go toward the costs of implementing the certification standards. However, these expenses may be too high for the neediest farmers to afford.

 Words to Understand in This Chapter

constraint—something that limits or restricts.

detractor—someone who criticizes something or belittles its value.

paradoxically—showing qualities that seem to be in contradiction with each other.

pay lip service—to say you believe in something without actually doing anything to put that belief into practice.

Size Matters

The fair trade movement has traditionally emphasized small-scale producers. Fair Trade USA, however, has pushed for expansion of the fair trade label to plantations and factories. In large part, this issue was behind Fair Trade USA's 2011 break with FairTrade International. Critics of Fair Trade USA argue that it is hard to maintain the same ethical standards while working with large-scale plantations. They also worry that sourcing ingredients from big plantations will put the squeeze on small-scale farmers, since they can't compete at the same economies of scale.

The new Fair Trade USA system also introduced a rule allowing multi-ingredient products to carry the fair trade certification label as long as they include a 25 percent minimum of fair trade ingredients. This means that a chocolate bar can be labeled "fair trade" as long as a quarter of its sugar content is fair trade—even if none of the chocolate itself is made from fair trade cocoa. Such policies, critics argue, dilute the meaning of the fair trade label and make it difficult for consumers to distinguish between products that reflect stronger and weaker fair trade standards. The bottom line for ethically minded consumers? Read the label carefully.

Europe is the world's biggest market for fair trade coffee. An estimated 75–80 percent of the world's certified fair trade coffee is distributed in shops, offices, and restaurants across Europe.

Moreover, as we saw in chapter 2, the fair trade system requires producers to be organized into cooperatives. This may be an obstacle for very poor, small-scale farmers, whose limited resources can make it difficult to form effective organizations.

Because of the costs and difficulties associated with the certification process, critics argue that the farmers most likely to become certified are middle-income producers with greater assets. Yet they are not the ones most in need of help. In 2007, for example, the countries with the greatest number of fair trade–certified coffee producers—Mexico, Colombia, Peru, and South Africa—had an average per capita GDP of $4,790. By contrast, the thirteen nations with only one certified coffee producer had an average per capita GDP of just $2,807. Coffee-producing nations without any fair trade–certified producers at all had even lower GDPs.

Growing the Market

Fair trade sales represent a very small share of the market—less than 1 percent. This small size means that fair trade can have, at best, only a very limited impact on the global economy. And, according to some critics, the costs and requirements involved in becoming certified are *constraints* on the movement's ability to expand, limiting its reach to a tiny fraction of the developing world's producers.

But tiny as the fair trade market may be, fair trade sales represent one of the fastest-growing segments of the global food market. Since 1998, sales of fair trade products have shot up at an average of 30–40 percent almost every year. Even during the financial crisis of 2008, fair trade sales recorded a highly

 Did You Know?

Fairtrade International grants half of the seats in its twenty-four-seat General Assembly to producer organizations. This means that producers in the Global South have a 50 percent say in the governance of the organization. This contrasts with the nonegalitarian structure of the World Bank and the IMF, where votes are allocated on the basis of nations' incomes.

respectable growth rate of 22 percent. In some countries, fair trade products have already captured a significant share of the market. In Switzerland, for example, fair trade bananas enjoy a 50 percent market share.

Paradoxically, however, the rapid growth of the movement has led some fair trade activists to worry about the direction it is going in.

Corporations and Fair Trade

In recent years, as the fair trade movement has demonstrated that there is a growing consumer market for more ethically sourced goods, large multinational corporations have moved to cash in. In 2000, facing protests over alleged labor rights violations on its coffee plantations, Starbucks started stocking fair trade coffee. Coca-Cola sells fair trade tea–based beverages under the brand name Honest Tea. And consumers can even find a range of fair trade products on the shelves of Walmart, a massive corporate empire that has repeatedly come under fire for its poor labor practices at home.

Critics argue that these large companies are simply capitalizing on the good reputation of the fair trade movement while paying no more than *lip service* to its real goals. Typically, fair trade goods make up only a tiny portion of the overall product line of big corporate retailers. For example, in 2010 Starbucks reported that only 8 percent of its coffee beans were certified as fair trade. Moreover, the trend is for corporations to develop their own labeling initiatives—based on requirements that are a watered-down

The ABCs of Fair Trade

Navigating the different organizational layers of the fair trade movement can be confusing. The acronyms alone may seem like alphabet soup. Here are some of the most prominent organizations:

- Fairtrade Labelling Organization International (FLO) was created in 1997 to establish a unified set of standards for labeling and certification. In 2009, FLO split into two wings: Fairtrade International, which identifies the standards and requirements that fair trade companies and producers must follow, and FLO-CERT, which inspects and certifies products to ensure that they meet the standards. Confusingly, Fairtrade International still goes by the old acronym, FLO.

- The World Fair Trade Organization (WFTO) is an international association of fair trade organizations. Its members include producer cooperatives, importers, retailers, and national and regional fair trade networks. The WFTO has its own label, the FTO mark. But while the FLO label is applied to products, the FTO mark is applied to organizations. It designates organizations with a 100 percent fair trade commitment.

- The Network of European Worldshops (NEWS!), formed in 1994, is an association of worldshop associations across Europe. Worldshops are specialized retail outlets, usually nonprofits, that sell fair trade products and are often active in social justice causes.

- FINE is an informal association of fair trade federations. Created in 1998, it works to strengthen fair trade standards, improve monitoring and oversight, and advocate for fair trade in the political arena.

A group of Indian workers listen as a representative of Pushpanjali, a fair trade organization based in Agra, speaks about health insurance.

version of the original fair trade standards. This, critics warn, has the potential to weaken fair trade standards across the board.

Meanwhile, these big corporations are crowding out small companies that show a genuine commitment to fair trade ideals—companies such as Planet Bean Coffee, La Siembra, and JustUs! All three of these companies—pioneers from the early days of Canada's fair trade movement—are socially conscious, worker-owned cooperatives that sell only 100 percent fair trade products. They pay farmers well above the fair trade minimum price. And they are dedicated to promoting fairer labor rights back home, too.

The Future of Fair Trade

Critics raise important concerns about how corporations are impacting the broader fair trade movement. Yet the mainstreaming of the fair trade movement has also brought some positive results. On the plus side, the involvement of big corporations has increased the volume of fair trade sales. In 2011, worldwide sales surpassed $6 billion. These sales have added billions of dollars to the incomes of farmers in the developing world.

Thanks to the broader reach of big companies, fair trade products are now much more widely available across North America. Starbucks alone, for example, has almost eight thousand stores in the United States and Canada. Although 8 percent may be a small fraction of its overall coffee supply, in absolute numbers, this amounts to a greater turnover of fair trade beans than small companies can claim. And

The American company Starbucks operates over 17,000 stores in more than forty countries, including this shop in Tokyo, Japan. The company, which sells an estimated 4 million cups of coffee every day, has embraced fair trade standards.

with their big-brand power, corporations like Starbucks can raise the public profile of the movement.

Will working with mainstream markets and big corporations like Starbucks and Walmart erode fair trade standards? The future of fair trade remains to be seen. The movement is still evolving. But seventy years after Edna Ruth Byler sold her first fair trade textiles in small-town Kansas, at least one thing is clear: the ideal of socially responsible trade is here to stay.

From the early days of handicrafts sold in car trunks and church basements, the fair trade movement has come a long way. Fair trade has helped to lift hundreds of thousands of small-scale producers out of the worst conditions of poverty. It has brought an awareness of global inequalities into the mainstream consciousness. And the movement continues to prompt consumers in the West to think about where their dollars go and how their shopping habits affect the lives of farmers and other producers on the other side of the world. Fair trade is not a substitute for more comprehensive approaches to poverty reduction, but it may well be one important part of the solution.

 ## Text-Dependent Questions

1. Why do some critics argue that fair trade doesn't benefit the world's neediest farmers?
2. What are some of the criticisms of corporate involvement in the fair trade movement?
3. What are some positive effects of corporate involvement in the fair trade movement?

 ## Research Project

Fair trade standards oppose the use of genetically modified organisms (GMOs). Some critics argue that this approach is harmful to producers because genetic engineering can sometimes lead to improvements in farming—especially in the case of bananas, which are sterile and highly prone to disease. Conduct some independent research on the pros and cons of GMOs. Based on what you learn, write a report stating whether you think that the fair trade prohibition against GMOs is justified or not.

Chronology

1944   The World Bank and the International Monetary Association are created at a meeting in Bretton Woods, New Hampshire.

1946   Kansas businesswoman Edna Ruth Byler begins selling hand-sewn textiles from Puerto Rico to help disadvantaged artisans, an initiative that eventually morphs into the well-known fair trade retail outlet Ten Thousand Villages.

1947   The General Agreement on Tariffs and Trade (GATT) is established to set rules for international trade and oversee trade negotiations between nations.

1948   Oxfam, a nonprofit working on issues of poverty, hunger, and global justice, opens its first charity shop to sell fair trade products.

1988   Solidaridad partners with UCIRI coffee growers, resulting in the Max Havelaar certification label, the world's first fair trade consumer label.

1989   The World Fair Trade Organization (WFTO) is created as an international umbrella association of fair trade organizations.

1994   The Network of European Worldshops (NEWS!), an association of European fair trade worldshops, is formed. The United States, Canada, and Mexico form the North American Free Trade Agreement (NAFTA).

1995   The World Trade Organization is created, taking over the functions of GATT.

1997   The Fairtrade Labelling Organization International (FLO) is created to establish a unified set of standards for labeling and certification.

1998   FINE, an association of fair trade federations, is created.

2000   Starbucks starts selling fair trade certified coffee in its stores.

2001   The United States adopts the Harkin-Engel Protocol, a voluntary agreement to eradicate child labor from the chocolate industry.

2004   The WFTO launches its own label, certifying fair trade organizations.

2009   FLO splits into Fairtrade International, which identifies the fair trade certification standards, and FLO-CERT, which inspects and certifies products to ensure that they meet the standards.

2011   Fair Trade USA becomes independent from Fairtrade International.

Organizations to Contact

FairTrade Canada
1145 Carling Ave., Suite 7500
Ottawa, Ontario
Canada K17 7K4
Phone: +1-613-563-3351
Email: info@fairtrade.ca
Website: www.fairtrade.ca

FairTrade International (FLO)
Bonner Talweg 177
53129 Bonn
Germany
Phone: +49-228-949230
Fax: +49-228-2421713
Email: info@fairtrade.net
Website: www.fairtrade.net

Fair Trade USA
1500 Broadway #400
Oakland, CA 94612
Phone: 510-663-5260
Fax: 510-663-5264
Website: www://fairtradeusa.org

World Fair Trade Organization (WFTO)
Godfried Bomansstraat 8-3
4103 WR Culemborg
The Netherlands
Phone: +31 (0) 345-53-64-87
Email: info@wfto.com
Website: www.wfto.com

World Trade Organization (WTO)
Centre William Rappard
Rue de Lausanne 154
CH-1211 Geneva 21
Switzerland
Phone: +41 (0)22 739-5111
Fax: +41 (0)22 731-4206
Email: enquiries@wto.org
Website: www.wto.org

Organisation for Economic Co-operation and Development (OECD)
Washington Centre
2001 L Street, NW, Suite 650,
Washington, DC 20036-4922
Phone: (202) 785-6323
Fax: (202) 785-0350
E-mail: washington.contact@oecd.org
Website: www.oecd.org

US Chamber of Commerce
1615 H Street, NW
Washington, DC 20062
Phone: (202) 659-6000
Fax: (202) 463-3126
Email: Americas@uschamber.com
Website: www.uschamber.com

Series Glossary

barter—the official department that administers and collects the duties levied by a government on imported goods.

bond—a debt investment used by companies and national, state, or local governments to raise money to finance projects and activities. The corporation or government borrows money for a defined period of time at a variable or fixed interest rate.

credit—the ability of a customer to obtain goods or services before payment, based on the trust that payment will be made in the future.

customs—the official department that administers and collects the duties or tariffs levied by a government on imported goods.

debt—money, or something else, that is owed or due in exchange for goods or services.

demurrage—extra charges paid to a ship or aircraft owner when a specified period for loading or unloading freight has been exceeded.

distributor—a wholesaler or middleman engaged in the distribution of a category of goods, esp to retailers in a specific area.

duty—a tax on imported goods.

export—to send goods or services to another country for sale.

Federal Reserve—the central bank of the United States, which controls the amount of money circulating in the US economy and helps to set interest rates for commercial banks.

import—to bring goods or services into a country from abroad for sale.

interest—a fee that is paid in exchange for the use of money that has been borrowed, or for delaying the repayment of a debt.

stock—an ownership interest in a company. Stocks are sold by companies to raise money for their operations. The price of a successful company's stock will typically rise, which means the person who originally bought the stock can sell it and earn a profit.

tariff—a government-imposed tax that must be paid on certain imported or exported goods.

value added tax (VAT)—a type of consumption tax that is placed on a product whenever value is added at each stage of production and at final sale. VAT is often used in the European Union.

World Bank—an international financial organization, connected to the United Nations. It is the largest source of financial aid to developing countries.

Further Reading

DeCarlo, Jacqueline. *Fair Trade and How It Works*. New York: Rosen Publishing, 2011.

Driscoll, William J., and Julie Clark. *Globalization and the Poor: Exploitation or Equalizer?* New York: International Debate Education Association, 2003.

Haugen, David M., and Rachael Mach. *Globalization*. Detroit: Greenhaven Press, 2010.

Hunt, Jilly. *Fair Trade*. Chicago: Heinemann Library, 2012.

Johanson, Paula. *Making Good Choices about Fair Trade*. New York: Rosen Central, 2010.

Powell, Jillian. *Fair Trade*. London: Wayland, 2012.

Young, Mitchell. *Free Trade*. Detroit: Greenhaven Press, 2009.

Internet Resources

http://data.worldbank.org

The World Bank's searchable database provides a wealth of statistics on economic growth, poverty, trade, environmental impacts, and many other topics on a country-by-country basis.

http://hdr.undp.org/en/reports

The website of the United Nations Development Programme offers country profiles, in-depth reports, and statistical data on topics related to human development, including economic indicators.

http://comtrade.un.org

This repository of detailed global trade data gives you free access to official trade statistics from the United Nations, going back to 1962.

www.fairtradefederation.org

The website of the Fair Trade Federation, an association of Canadian and American wholesalers, importers, and retailers, is a clearinghouse for information on fair trade.

Publisher's Note: The websites listed on this page were active at the time of publication. The publisher is not responsible for websites that have changed their address or discontinued operation since the date of publication. The publisher reviews and updates the websites each time the book is reprinted.

http://fairtradeusa.org
http://fairtrade.ca/

The homepages of Fair Trade USA and FairTrade Canada provide detailed fact sheets about fair trade products and the farmers and workers who produce them, along with information about the fair trade movement and links to resources for consumers.

www.globalexchange.org/resources

The "Resources" page of the Global Exchange website offers a wealth of information on global economics and specific economic issues facing different regions around the world.

www.inequality.org

A project of the Institute of Policy Studies, this information-packed site provides reports, fact sheets, suggestions for related readings, and links to resources and organizations related to world inequality.

Index

Numbers in ***bold italic*** refer to captions.

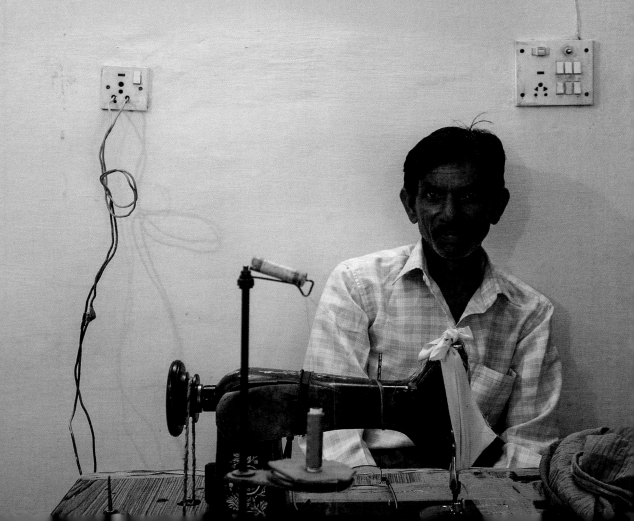

About the Author

Elisabeth Herschbach is an editor and writer from Maryland. Her other books for a middle school audience include *Lower Plains: Kansas, Nebraska* (Mason Crest, 2015) and *Lobbyists and Special Interest Groups* (Eldorado Ink, 2016).